Jill was born in Essex in 1948, and moved to Wandsworth with her parents and older sister not long after. She later moved to the Isle of Wight with her mother and sister for three years, before returning to Wandsworth in 1963. Jill is married, with three daughters, two grandsons, and an elderly cat called Boody, and has lived in East Sussex for just over forty years. She qualified as a British Wheel of Yoga teacher in 1991, and was awarded a Diploma in Counselling in 1995, then worked for twelve years as a Group Leader and Counsellor at a drop-in Centre for Mental Health Service Users. She studied Creative Writing at Sussex University, and was awarded an MA in Creative Writing, The Arts & Education in 2003. Jill is devoted to cats and works part-time at the National Cat Adoption Centre in Chelwood Gate, in addition to providing holiday cover for other Yoga teachers.

JILL CLARK

A Life in
BLACK & WHITE

First published in Great Britain as a softback original in 2019

Copyright © Jill Clark

The moral right of this author has been asserted.

All rights reserved.

No part of this publication may be reproduced, stored in a retrieval system, or transmitted, in any form or by any means, without the prior permission in writing of the publisher, nor be otherwise circulated in any form of binding or cover other than that in which it is published and without a similar condition including this condition being imposed on the subsequent purchaser.

Typeset in Minion Pro

Design, typesetting and publishing by UK Book Publishing

www.ukbookpublishing.com

ISBN: 978-1-913179-39-7

A Life in
BLACK & WHITE

DEDICATION

This book is dedicated to the late Gem Groombridge, who was my yoga teacher, mentor and very good friend for many years. She gave me unconditional love, support and encouragement, and helped me to believe in myself, and to develop as a person.

ACKNOWLEDGEMENTS

I would like to thank my husband Peter for his steadfast support and encouragement, without which this book would never have come into being. I would also like to thank my three beautiful daughters, Cressida, Claire and Jemma, for their support, their valuable feedback and their patience, and my beloved sister Marion, better known as Melly, my nickname for her since childhood. She was my co-conspirator during the early years, although we didn't always like each other very much. However, blood is thicker than water, and our relationship has developed and grown into a beautiful thing. I cannot begin to express what you all mean to me.

CONTENTS

INTRODUCTION: 1
Metamorphosis 3
Dragon Slayer 4
Listen with Mother 5
Skiffle 6
Pleasures 7
Thirst 8
Growing Pains 10
Shut Your Eyes 11
Black and White 12
Heated 13
Hospital Corners 14
Mad Scramble 15
All at Sea 16
Absent Father 17
Redemption 19
District Line to Elm Park 20
Good Times 21
Durrington Towers – 1964 23
First Kiss 24
Dancing Queen 25
Virgo Man 27
Signal Failure 28
Breaking the News 29
Gretna Green: November 1968 30
Baby Blues 32
Baby Blues II 34
South Croydon 1972 35
Modern Lullaby 37

SECOND TIME AROUND: **38**
No love lost 39
Not that One 40
Cyprus 2013 41
Hard Cheese 42
Seeing Red 43

THE BLACK DOG: **44**
Flight 45
Black Dog 46

WORK: **47**
Marrowfat Peas 48

FOR SUE: 27th April 1949 – 1st SEPTEMBER 2015 .... **49**
January 2016 50
A Year On 51
Eighteen Months Later 52
Two Years On 53
October 2018 – Ghost 54
February 2019 – Snow Angel 55

BALL AND CHAIN: **56**
Ball and Chain 57

BELIEF: **60**
Belief 61
A Grand Day Out 62

CONTENTS

FOR MY SISTER: 2019 ... **63**
Big Sister ... 64

OTHER STUFF: ... **66**
Pipe Dream ... 67
Picture This ... 68
Nerine ... 69
Samaritan ... 70
Charlie: Postscript to Black & White ... 72
Aurora ... 73

ENDINGS: ... **74**
Rest in Peace ... 75
V Sign ... 76
Bearhug ... 77
Last Photo ... 78
The Magic Book ... 79

APPENDIX ... **89**
Italian Beach by A.J. Smith ... 90

INTRODUCTION:

I was in my early forties when my friend Gem suggested that it might be beneficial for me to see a counsellor, as she knew that I have struggled with feelings of worthlessness and insecurity my entire life, resulting in episodes of deep depression.

Subsequently, a counsellor helped me to unlock the feelings and emotions buried inside me, and to express them in a safe environment, starting me on a journey of self-discovery, which continues to this day. I wrote my first poem ever, **Dragon Slayer**, during this period, after watching the film "Robin Hood: Prince of Thieves," because the Sheriff of Nottingham's mother Mortianna, who was portrayed as an evil witch, triggered terrifying and powerful memories of my childhood.

Many of my poems are about my relationship with my Mother. It has been a painful and cathartic process which has helped me to find my voice, and to move on. I am quite sure that my Mum suffered from an undiagnosed mental illness, which was exacerbated by the loss of her firstborn, my sister Jean, who died in a horrific accident when she was six. My father was abroad, fighting for his country during World War II, and it took him over a month to return home on compassionate leave. Unfortunately, there was no such thing as counselling in those days; you just had to keep a stiff upper lip, and get on with it.

Although my poems don't show Mum in a positive light, I am very grateful to her for bringing me up with a sense of right and wrong, and good old-fashioned moral values. I know that she did the best she could, under extremely difficult circumstances.

INTRODUCTION

I have called this collection of poetry and prose **Black & White**, not only as a reference to one of my poems with the same title, which was inspired by a black & white photo, but also, because much of my work is written from a child's perspective, and it is normal for children to see and express their world in terms of extremes, i.e., black or white, good or bad. Developmental psychologists call this polarization 'primitive thinking,' and believe that most adults are prone to regressing to primitive thinking when they are having a hard time, or are feeling overwhelmed by their emotions.

Several of my poems have a fairy tale motif, as I am particularly interested in fairy tales and the way in which they portray existential dilemmas, and also reflect cultural and social norms at the time they were written. I have included a modern take on a fairy tale I wrote some years ago, at the end of the collection.

My first poem, **Metamorphosis**, is an exploration of the mother/daughter relationship, using ideas taken from the story of Red Riding Hood. It was inspired by a doll my youngest daughter was given many years ago. At one end, is Red Riding Hood, complete with red cloak. At the other, underneath Red Riding Hood's full skirt, grandma and the wolf are neatly combined as a Janus face under a mob cap, looking in opposite directions, so grandma represents the positive, nurturing aspect of human nature, and the wolf represents the negative, destructive aspect. If we look at the main characters in the story according to Freudian theory, the mother/grandma figure represents the Superego, and the Wolf, the Id, whilst according to the Jungian theory of archetypes, the grandma figure represents the Wise Woman, and the Wolf, the Shadow self.

The poem certainly reflects my own confusing and unhappy experience of growing up with a mother who could be caring and loving, but also extremely volatile and frightening.

Metamorphosis

I should feel safe in the cottage,
with the stout wooden door
firmly bolted.

You sit by the fire
rocking me to sleep,
your warm lap a refuge
from the gathering shadows,
a lullaby on your lips.

But my dreams bring no
comfort, for lying beneath the
soft folds of your skirt,
the wolf is waiting.

Her snarling jaws eager
to tear out my heart,
should I lose the cloak,
drop the basket,
or spill the wine.

Oh mother what big teeth you've got.
All the better to eat you with my dear,
A stain like blood on your lips
as you slowly stoop to kiss me.

Dragon Slayer

Where were you, my knight
in shining armour, when
Mortianna with the crazy eyes
stormed through the house,
filled me with terror, turned
me to stone with a glance.

If it was a good day
she'd sing me lullabies,
stroke my hair as we lay
together in her big double bed,
our bodies curved, moulding as
snugly as two spoons in a drawer.

Perhaps you didn't know what
she was really like, passed it
off as a woman living on her
nerves, felt you had no choice,
when you left me there alone,
slaying all the dragons.

Listen with Mother

It's almost time.
My mother takes her place
in the sagging armchair by the fire.
I climb into the warm hammock
her skirt makes, snuggle closer until
there is no space between us, and
listen to the soft thump of her heart as
it beats a faint tattoo against my cheek.

Are you sitting comfortably?
Then I'll begin.
The music starts, as familiar
and soothing as her strong arms
around me. My eyelids grow
heavy and I drift off to sleep,
too young to realise
I'll never feel this safe again.

Skiffle

Sometimes there are jam sessions.
Uncle Alan plays the guitar,
Uncle Stan slaps the spoons
against his thigh, and Dad
plays the washboard with the
metal thimble my mother wears
when she is sewing late into the night.

Sometimes when Dad is at work
she explodes without warning,
hits me hard with the cane,
pulls me by my hair onto my
knees until I end up sprawled
across the red flagstones, feeling
the toe of her soft pink slipper.

Pleasures

We both crouch down behind the
Wendy house. *You go first,* my sister
says, keeping a lookout for grown-ups.
She watches the warm stream of pee
spurt from that forbidden place.

It splashes my bare toes and Clarks
sandals, turns the parched earth to
mud. Ants scurry from the rivulets
like the people I once saw in a film,
escaping from molten lava.

Afterwards we dig in the flowerbed,
giggling as we make each other dinner.
Grass, dirt and mashed up rose petals.
The coconut matting tickles our legs
when we sit on the floor, pretending to eat.

I pick up a fat worm and watch it
wriggle, tunnelling through air.
My sister screams when I chase her,
knowing she'll get her own back
with a Chinese burn, after lights out.

Thirst

My mother sings as we walk along the path
through the woods, her voice drowning out
the soft murmur of trees, a good sign.
Lavender's blue, dilly dilly, lavender's green,
When I am king, dilly dilly, you will be queen

Sometimes she changes the words to
Lavender's blue, Jilly Jilly, lavender's green,
When I am king Jilly Jilly, you will be queen
and everything in my world is alright.

My sister and I snatch at bluebells,
competing to see who can pick the biggest
bunch, balance on fallen branches across the
stream, crocodiles snapping at our feet.

When we get home Mum puts the bluebells
in her favourite vase and places it on the
chest-of-drawers in our bedroom.
She won it playing hoopla at the fair,
eyes shining up at Dad, her mouth
as round as the hoop she'd just thrown.

In the morning, she finds them scattered,
wilting in the early sun. *Who did this?*
she shouts, reaching for the hard wooden
hairbrush. *It was Jilly,* my sister says,
quick to point the finger. *She got up in the*
middle of the night and drank all the water.

I don't remember doing it, but my mother
sees the funny side of it, thank God.

Growing Pains

She told us not to let her down by
behaving like *those common children
who climbed people's walls,
screamed loudly, got dirty.*

She loved her precious plants and flowers.
*There goes the lady with the beautiful
garden and the two lovely girls*
the neighbours said.

She gave me fat bunches
of fragrant syringa, velvet
petalled roses, picked before
breakfast, to give to the teacher.

The other children laughed,
called me *teacher's pet*. I tried
to impress them, acted the fool,
got sent to the headmistress.

Back home my sister teased me.
You fucking cow I shouted,
not sure what it meant, but
enjoying the feeling of power.

My mother took hold of my ear,
dragged me to the sink.
Lifebuoy household soap.
I can taste it now.

Shut Your Eyes

My mother used to suffer from terrible
headaches. I'd try to comfort her, knowing
she was vulnerable and needed taking care of.
I would tell her, *Shut your eyes and pretend
it's not there,* which was my way of dealing
with things which hurt me.

It was a strategy I developed in order to survive.
I learnt to put on a brave face, to swallow my
feelings, so nothing could get through to me,
laying the foundations for a way of being that
was totally incongruent, but felt safe.

Shut your eyes and pretend it's not there.
The fact that I was ugly and stupid,
a failure, a bad girl to boot, until I
finally realised that I'd wasted far too
much of my life believing she was right.

Black and White

Jilly stares into the camera
holding her beloved cat
(who will later go missing)
like a baby in her arms.

She is wearing a sailcloth skirt,
white ric rac around the hem.
The last thing her mother made
before losing most of her sight.

*A rare condition triggered by
complications during pregnancy,*
her mother once told her.
*But I don't regret having you,
not for one moment.*

The crease in Jilly's forehead
and the droop of her mouth;
surely she already understands
the weight of her debt.

Heated

My mother calls from the kitchen.
She stands there in her petticoat,
sweat gathering like tears
between her breasts.

She pushes back her hair with floury
fingers, leaves white smudges on her face.
She slices the golden crust from the bread,
spreads it thickly with oily butter and
home-made blackberry jam.

The bittersweet taste stings my tongue,
reminds me of a cold Autumn day.
Bramble-scratched knees, red
fingerprints on the back of my leg.
For goodness sake, get a move on.

Hospital Corners

It's Monday.
Bright flutter of virgin sheets
heralding failure, my fingers
clumsy as, fresh from the line,
the ritual commences.

First we fold, pinch the corners
together tightly and pull diagonally,
first to the left, then to the right.
*For God's sake, don't drop it,
can't you do anything properly?*

When I help her change the beds
it all begins again. Sheets stretched
tight, as smooth as icing on a cake.
But my corners don't pass muster,
however hard I try. She curls her lip,
rips the sheet off. *You can bloody well
do it again, until you get it right.*

Mad Scramble

Her voice is brittle with expectation,
chalk scraping on a blackboard.
Come on you two, let's have a mad scramble.
She says it with an air of gaiety
like she's offering a treat;
a trip to the zoo maybe,
or a picnic in the park.
My heart plummets, knowing
we're in for a rough ride.
A whole day of our summer holiday
spent cleaning, dusting, sorting clothes.
A myriad of tasks to perform
and we're destined to fail.
I'd spin straw into gold for her
if only I knew how.

All at Sea

I stand on the groyne
with my mother and father
looking out to sea,
and slip, unnoticed.

The water closes silently over
me, filling my nose,
my mouth, my ears.
The taste of salt.

A hand clutches my hair, drags
me to the surface, coughing and
spluttering, a garland of
seaweed around my neck.

I look at my parents,
struck by their laughter.

Absent Father

You were absent even then.
I'd creep from my bed,
tiptoe along the corridor
and down the stairs, carefully
avoiding the one that squeaked.

If I was in luck
your brown raincoat
would be hanging there,
on the tall wooden coat
stand in the corner.

I'd wrap the sleeves around
me, bury my face in it.
Your smell.
Players Weights, Old Spice,
reassuring and familiar.

If it was Friday the pockets
bulged with sweets.
A quarter of jelly babies
or liquorice allsorts to
be shared with my sister.

I was so excited when you took me
to see *How the West Was Won*,
The Black and White Minstrel Show.
You said I was your special girl, but
you never asked if anything was wrong.

ABSENT FATHER

Years later I realised it was too late
when you lay on a hospital bed,
gasping like a stranded fish.
You didn't seem to know me,
absent for the last time.

Redemption

A child cries in the darkness.
Above the bed hangs a picture
of Jesus 'The Good Shepherd'
Suffer little children to come unto me.

Blue as forget-me-nots, his eyes
follow her, arms stretched wide in
embrace, hands with pearl fingernails,
as shiny as her mother's brooch.

She sinks to her knees on the cold lino.
*Dear God, please make me good
so that Mummy will love me and
Daddy will come back.*

She knows it's because she could
never live up to her perfect sister;
*An angel loaned by God
for the duration of the War.*

District Line to Elm Park

Once, on Christmas Eve, Mum sent my sister and
I to see our Nanny Wilton in Elm Park; a journey
on the District Line which seemed to take forever.
We were both still very young; Melly was probably
only about nine, so I would have been seven.
On the way back, a man kept leaning over us,
mumbling and slurring his words. I remember
feeling really scared, but nobody came to our rescue.

Melly made me get up and stand by the doors with
her, to make it look as if we were getting off. He
followed us, and suddenly lurched towards me.
I jumped back, dropping the jar of marmalade
Nanny had given me for Mum onto the floor, just
as he vomited right where I'd been standing. The
jar smashed, but we never told Mum, and I've
been terrified of drunk people ever since.

Good Times

I still have a black and white photo taken on the day Mum and Dad took us to the new outdoor Swimming Pool in St Georges Park. Mum looks as carefree and glamorous as a 1950's starlet in her one-piece swimsuit, Dad looks debonair in his black trunks, whilst my sister and I look bedraggled in our horrible ruched cozzies, which were very popular at the time, but quickly became waterlogged and slid down below our nipples when we went in the pool. We're standing in the blue, octagonal cascade fountain. It had three tiers and I remember sitting on the middle one behind a curtain of flowing water, thinking no-one could see me.

Then, a few years later, "Uncle" Bob occasionally took Mum, Melly and me for a drive in the country in his Austin 1100. I usually fell asleep within minutes. Mum would turn round in her seat and say brightly, *Why don't you wake up and look at the lovely scenery, Jilly?* It was as if she thought I was doing it on purpose. Bob always stopped at a pub on the way home. Melly and I would be locked in the car, clutching a bottle of pop and a bag of crisps with a twist of salt in blue waxed paper, thinking that all our Christmases had come at once.

I remember the time Mum took us to Cranleigh, the place where she and Jean were evacuated during World War II. We caught a train, just the three of us, then hiked through woods, over fields, and along quiet country lanes edged with Queen Anne's lace, which looked very pretty but stank of cats pee. At lunchtime, we sat on fallen logs and ate our picnic, sucking so hard on the frozen Jubblies Mum had bought for us as a treat that we both had brain freeze. It hurt like hell. Afterwards, she took us skinny dipping in a "secret" pool to cool off because the sun was burning our skin. The ice-cold water took my breath away. Although I didn't like the feel of the slimy weeds wrapping themselves around my legs like the tentacles of some undiscovered monster, it was a magical day.

Another time, when I was about fifteen, I had to have a suspicious lump cut out of my right breast. Luckily it proved to be benign, but I was terribly sick when I came round from the anaesthetic. Mum visited me later, and brought a flask of fresh lemon cordial she'd made, especially for me. It tasted heavenly and soon settled my stomach. Because we often didn't see eye to eye, I remember feeling profoundly touched by her thoughtfulness.

Durrington Towers – 1964

The lift is scarred with graffiti
and stinks of urine.
I feel an iron band of pain
constricting my heart.

She opens the door, fixes a
tepid smile in place but you're
right behind her, a welcoming
beacon on stormy seas.

You make the best of it, pointing
out the advantages of living at such
dizzying heights, the splendid view
right across London.

All I can see, far below in the
dismal light, is a tangle of railway
lines, inextricably linked,
stretching into infinity.

(Visit to my father after he remarried)

First Kiss

I purse my lips and close
my eyes the way I've
seen Doris Day do it
in *Move over Darling*.

He grabs my shoulders,
grinds his mouth on mine,
pushing with his tongue until my lips
part, saliva dribbling down my chin.

He lets go suddenly, walks off quickly
as though nothing has happened,
while I try to cover the blotches
with my sister's Pan Stick.

Dancing Queen

I'm the centre of attention at the party,
loving every minute. I know I look
good in my short red dress, diamante
earrings and the black satin gloves
belonging to my mother.

Witty and vivacious
I dazzle and shine,
make them roar with laughter.
They hang on my every word,
hopelessly hooked.

I knock back my fifth gin and lime,
watch them watching me,
mesmerised by the swell of my
breasts in the push-up bra
as I lean towards them.

They're moving in for the kill.
I thrust my hips like Elvis,
twist and shake to The Beatles
remembering a time when
my father still lived with us.

He'd put on Porgy and Bess,
ask me to dance for him.
I'd be Margot Fonteyn, leaping and
twirling until the whole room spun.
Daddy clapped, so proud of me.

DANCING QUEEN

Look at me now, see how your
little girl has grown, sprawled on
coats in somebody's bedroom,
having sex with the first man
who asks, still proud of me?

Virgo Man

It starts badly when I tread
mud into your carpet.
You rush about hoovering,
the lines on your forehead,
deeper than ever.

I try not to spread myself out
too much, then break all the
rules by blurting I love you
as we lie together
on your bed.

You find fault with my orgasms,
0.4 on the Richter scale
(when I'm not faking it).
I feel like an experiment
which is going to fail.

I leave *Miss Dior* on the pillow,
lipstick on a coffee cup and
pubic hair in the bath.
Worse still, our lovemaking
taints your sheets.

You strip them,
throw the windows open,
and when I leave, I know
you'll wash away
every single trace of me.

Signal Failure

I still wave at trains.
The driver of the 10.08 to Victoria
toots his horn as it hurtles along
the track. I'm standing on the
railway bridge trying to get
through to you. Your voice is
distant, tinged with reproof, each
frugal word a gift to be savoured.
I'll phone you back tomorrow
you say, then hang up. I'm
giving you the green light
but you're still stuck on amber.
Proceed with due caution
and only on your terms.

Breaking the News

When I tell her she picks up the
cereal bowl, throws it across the
kitchen. I watch it smash
on the floor, milk pooling.

Her face is cold,
unmoved by my tears,
the roar of silence more
potent than any weapon.

She speaks at last.
*You stupid girl, you've proved
I'm right. I knew you'd come
to no good.*

I watch her lips spit out the words
like sharp cherry stones,
longing for her arms around
me, and then I fall.

When I come to, my head aches
but not as much as my heart,
for the unborn child
of a *slut* and a *whore*.

Gretna Green: November 1968

You can't go airing your dirty linen in public
my mother said, worried about what the
neighbours might think.
You know his parents will never agree.
You'll have to elope to Gretna Green.
I didn't know what to do
though he was all for it, so I went
with the majority, as always.

It was a bleak and desolate place in winter.
The leaden sky crushed down on
scarecrow trees, bent double,
impotent in the face of the wind.
It howled like a banshee,
slashed at my face and the backs of
my legs, the thin leather coat
no match for the numbing cold.

Three weeks in a dingy guesthouse
wondering if we'd be found out.
We could barely afford to eat.
The same menu night after night;
Lamb chop, roast chicken, or battered cod?
Not that I was able to face it.
How could something no bigger than a
small avocado make me feel so sick?

GRETNA GREEN: NOVEMBER 1968

My blue court shoes were falling off me
when finally we stood in the wooden
hut before a joyless registrar,
making promises he wouldn't keep.
Mum and Bob drove up from London
with Dad and Connie, a nice surprise.
I had high hopes then, I loved him,
but it was hardly the best day of my life.

Baby Blues

My first baby was over two weeks late
when they decided to induce me. First, a
doctor broke my water with a stainless
steel instrument a bit like a crochet
hook, then he inserted a drip into the back
of my hand. The midwife wasn't very keen
on husbands being present at the birth, but
Jerry refused to leave my side for a single
moment. We didn't know then that what
should have been a wonderful bonding
experience would break our relationship.
We were both so young and didn't have a clue.

The contractions started, wave after wave
of relentless pain, far worse than I could
ever have imagined. I felt as if I was being
eviscerated like William Wallace, the Scottish
patriot. I clung to Jerry's hand as I writhed on
the narrow bed, clamping my lips together to
stop myself screaming out loud. Every now and
then his white, anxious face would swim into view.
I remember how he tenderly stroked my hair
back from my forehead, told me that I didn't have
to be brave, it was okay to shout, but I'd been
brought up to be a good girl, to never make a fuss.

After several hours, the midwife said I was ready to push;
it was such a relief. With every push I could see blood
from the vein in my hand snaking back up the drip tube.
Jerry looked horrified when he spotted it. I thought that
I'd been torn apart when finally, the midwife placed our
beautiful daughter on my chest. She weighed 8lbs 3ozs and
was absolutely perfect. Jerry cradled her gently, tears in
his eyes, as the midwife stitched me up, saying *It's only
a small tear,* but God, it really hurt.

Baby Blues II

Cressida was almost three when I had my second baby, another daughter, 6lbs 12ozs. This time, my husband stayed in the waiting room. Such a shame, as the birth was much easier, like shelling a pea from a pod. Claire had delicate features and rosebud lips; she reminded me of a beautiful doll my parents gave me one Christmas. It was my favourite toy and I used to take it everywhere until they gave me a Teddy bear. Claire was 9 months old when Jerry moved out, after telling me that he'd been unfaithful, and although he still loved me, he didn't feel the same about me in a physical way, after the trauma of witnessing the birth.

South Croydon 1972

He was out screwing other women.
I took the children to stay with friends
then swallowed all the tablets
in the bottle as Melanie wailed
mournfully on the record player.

I carved up his LPs with a knife,
Bob Dylan, Joni Mitchell and Joan
Baez. With every stab, every cut
I wished it was his cheating heart.

At the hospital they told me off
for being stupid, pushed rubber
tubing down my throat. When I
woke up hours later I felt like shit.

He appeared at my bedside
mouthing words of concern but
offering nothing. He'd clearly
had time to make his mind up.

They sent me to Warlingham Park.
A woman sat on the floor moaning,
her skirt over her head, exposing
thin white legs and underwear.

Grey-faced people shuffled
aimlessly between rows of narrow
beds, separated only by the
width of a small locker.

SOUTH CROYDON 1972

A nurse went through my suitcase
as I filled out forms like a robot. When
my friend refused to leave me there,
I clung to her like a drowning woman.

Back home the silence was deafening.
I touched the empty spaces where his
things had been, sobbing as I burnt all
our photos, my dreams up in smoke.

Modern Lullaby

Oh hush thee my babie, thy sire was a knight.

Actually, he's a computer programmer at
IBM, and some bloody knight in shining
armour he turned out to be. Why in God's
name won't you go to sleep?

*Thy mother a lady both gentle and bright,
both gentle and bright.*

I know I look a mess, and I shouldn't cry
all the time, or get impatient with you.

*The woods and the glens from the towers
which we see, they all are belonging
dear babie to thee.*

We have a nice view of next door's overflowing
rubbish, a dirty old mattress and a rusty fridge,
but at least you have me, and I'll never leave
you, not like that lying, cheating bastard.

Oh hush thee my babie.........

NOW WILL YOU PLEASE STOP SCREAMING
AND GO TO SLEEP FOR MUMMY?

Italicised text taken from *"Lullaby of an infant chief"* by Sir Walter Scott, which my Mother sometimes sang to me at night. I sang it to my three babies in turn.

SECOND TIME AROUND:

I married my second husband in 1976, and as with all relationships, we have had our ups and downs. Somehow, we have managed to navigate through some very stormy waters, and have arrived at a place where we feel comfortable and at peace with each other. We still have our moments as we are naturally quite different in many ways; something John Gray expressed so succinctly in the title of his brilliant book "Men are from Mars, Women are from Venus. I know that I drive Peter mad at times, particularly as I have a habit of singing and humming constantly, or of falling asleep during an exciting thriller on TV, and then asking him what happened when I wake up. However, Peter and I both value the love, friendship and companionship we now share. I find that writing a poem about any "grievances" or issues that arise very cathartic, and it helps me to move on. Peter is my rock, and I would be lost without him.

No love lost

But love has been lost. It started so well; the
thrill I felt when you looked deep into my eyes,
all the things I thought we had in common. Long
conversations on the phone, lingering goodbyes
giggling on the doorstep, hot fast sex, slow
love-making. We could hardly bear to be apart.

We got married at Wandsworth Registry Office
during the heat wave of '76. I nearly melted in
the high-necked, long-sleeved dress I found in a
boutique on King's Road, proud to stand beside
you, so handsome and stylish in your kipper
tie and flares; a fine catch, everyone said.

Before long, the birth of our baby, both
in tears, thinking that this would cement
our relationship, but gradually the arguments
started, years of fighting and making up,
you slowly changing, withdrawing,
concerned with far weightier matters.

Yes, I changed too, had counselling,
took a course in assertiveness, began
to discover who I was for the first time.
You clearly felt threatened, didn't want
to talk about it, said I was being over-
analytical, so I stopped trying.

Not that One

No, not that carriage, even though the doors
have opened right in front of us, then off you
stroll whilst I follow meekly, wishing you would
hurry, aware of the guard's impatient whistle.

*No, not those seats, it's best to face the
direction we're travelling in,* so we walk
back down the carriage and end up where
we would have been in the first place.

No, not that queue, this one is shorter,
when we get to Victoria and I want a
cappuccino, so we get stuck behind the
person whose card doesn't work/is one
sandwich short of a picnic/doesn't speak
English/or the barista is going all out
for the Guinness Book of Records as
the slowest ever, take your pick.

Cyprus 2013

It's a balmy evening, our first in
Northern Cyprus. Over dinner, I
try out my Turkish on the friendly
waiter who says he will teach
me more words. You smile,
pleased I haven't forgotten.

We sip wine and gaze up at the sky.
It looks like a piece of black velvet,
scattered with sparkling sequins.
Flushed with wine and my earlier
success, I make an innocent remark,
something to do with my childhood.

Here we go again, you sigh
changing the mood in an instant,
then try to pass it off as a joke
when you see the expression
on my face. I stare at you, wondering
what happened to the man I married.

Hard Cheese

I'm moaning down the phone to my sister.
Our 37th anniversary and, once again,
no flowers. A lovely card, yes, but
not a flower in sight or anything else
for that matter. On our 30th a friend
asked me *So, how are you going to
celebrate? We went to the Maldives.*
I'm not asking for much. A book of
poetry, surprise picnic or breakfast in
bed would just about knock my socks off.

My niece is talking in the background,
clearly au fait with the complexities
of marriage. *Even a nice fresh
piece of Edam goes stale. You just
have to scrape off the mould and
get on with it.* I ponder on these
pearls of wisdom, after I've finished
laughing. There's a lot of truth in what
she says, and I realise that's just what
I've been doing, all these years.

Seeing Red

I suppose I shouldn't complain.
After all, you did make me a lovely
card with a sonnet by Shakespeare,
together with a bunch of flowers,
but they withered and died after
only three days, as dry and dusty as
poor Miss Havisham's trousseau.
I wondered if that was symbolic;
a metaphor for what we are
left with forty years on. A very
modest piece of jewellery in
recognition of loyal service would
have been nice, and if it had
featured a ruby, however tiny, I'd
have been totally gobsmacked.

THE BLACK DOG:

I have suffered from depression for most of my life. I can even remember standing on the cliff edge at Freshwater Bay, Isle of Wight, aged 12, feeling desperately unhappy and wishing I had the courage to throw myself off. Freud's theory of Thanatos postulates that all people have an unconscious desire to die, but the life instincts largely temper this wish. I seldom feel as bad as that anymore, although the black dog continues to walk beside me, and can overwhelm me if life becomes particularly stressful, sometimes taking me completely by surprise.

Flight

There's been a scratching noise for
days. *It's only mice*, you laugh.
Finally I unscrew the air vent
in the bricked-up fireplace.

I peer into the narrow space,
no bigger than a letterbox.
The jackdaw flaps sooty wings
when I lift him through.

As I wrap him in a towel
I feel his heart stuttering,
offer him moistened bread.
He gulps convulsively.

I go into the garden, gently
release him, laughter bubbling as
he takes flight, soaring high over
the rooftops, free once more.

Later, leaden with despair
I sit in the kitchen
trying to make sense of it all.
The minutes drag.

Anger rises, hot and bitter,
like bile in my throat. I walk
over to the window, and beat
my hands against the glass.

Black Dog

Black as night, he scratches at the door.
He's been skulking in the shadows
for over a week, but now he's growing
bolder, creeping closer every day.
Like a jealous lover, he wants me
for himself. If I let him in, he'll sink
his claws into me, pin me to the bed,
lies dripping like honey from his tongue.
Let's stay here for a while, you know
you're safe with me. Nobody understands
you like I do. What's the point in trying?
You never were much good at anything,
and I'm his for the taking.

WORK:

I worked as a Counsellor and Group Leader at a Drop-In Centre for mental health service users between 1994 and 2003. I was in awe of the service users' resilience in the face of enduring mental illness, even though they were often rejected by their families and by society. It was challenging work, and I wrote the poem **Marrowfat Peas** during this period.

I also ran a series of Creative Writing Workshops for service users, with three or four regular members who came when they felt well enough. There was a lot of laughter and fun, and the service users were very enthusiastic. I was really impressed with the quality of the work they produced, which was often insightful and moving, although it was occasionally somewhat "X-Rated!"

Marrowfat Peas

You're as bad as all the fucking rest.
You...
don't...
give...
a...
fuck...
about...
me...
he screams,
punctuating his anger
with the tin in his hand.
I stare at the dents in the table,
tongue heavy in my mouth,
sifting through words carefully.

Somehow I find the right thing to say
and he slumps in his chair.
Thanks for listening he says,
already moving on to the next crisis
whilst I sit on my hands to stop them shaking.

FOR SUE: 27TH APRIL 1949 – 1ST SEPTEMBER 2015

In loving memory of a truly free spirit

January 2016

I think about you every day,
remembering the fun we used to have;
the time we climbed up Black Cap in the dark
with only a torch to guide us because
I told you I'd never seen a glow-worm.
You suddenly stopped and said
"Listen, can you hear the nightingale?"
You taught me so much about nature,
and the magic of the world around us.

Everywhere I look there are reminders of you; gifts you
gave me for birthdays and Xmas, exquisitely wrapped,
label signed with a flamboyant flourish, *Very much love,
Sue*. The friendship ball in shades of blue, iridescent in the
light, quirky black metal sheep, lotus candle, dragonfly
fairy lights, the Poi spinning set which I never quite
got the hang of, and finally, your last gift, the beautiful
wooden box with a tree carving on the lid; inside, a
polished sandstone heart, engraved with a flower.

I hold the stone in the palm of my hand,
rub my fingers over the cold smooth surface,
thinking that you might just as well have
ripped my heart out and put it in a box
when you decided to take your own life.

A Year On

It's been a whole year since you left.
The faded pink ribbon tied to the stile
hangs forlornly, barely stirring in the wind.
I touch it, as I always do, before crossing
the railway track, trying not to focus on the
place where you laid yourself down
because then I will have to think about
how you must have felt in those last
few devastating moments of your life.

I try instead to remember the fun we had
tobogganing down Blackcap on a tin tray,
or walking on the Downs, your parrot Gus
perched on your shoulder like a modern day
Long John Silver; the time I hurled my baking
tray over the hedge as we walked down the
road after the Book Group Xmas Supper; a
grand gesture because I was fed up with
cooking. You couldn't believe I'd done it and
we laughed all the way home.

I could eulogise about your wonderful
qualities, try to canonise you, even admit
that yes, sometimes I found you hard work,
but all I really want is to tell you what is in my
heart, how much I love and miss you and wish
that I had been a better friend.

Eighteen Months Later

The last time I saw you was in the Post Office of all places.
I threw my arms around you, not knowing I'd never
see your caring face, or hear your voice again.
You asked me if I fancied a trip to India, later in the
year, and I said *Let's get together and talk about it soon,*
even though I wasn't sure I wanted to spend two weeks
with you that far away from home, as I sometimes
found your searching questions and frenetic energy quite
exhausting. I am so glad now that I didn't hesitate, not
even for a moment, and wish I could tell you that
I'd go to India with you in a heartbeat, if only I could.

Two Years On

Two years now, and I don't know
what else there is to say. Life goes on
of course, but I still miss you, so I try
not to think about you too often.
There are so many things I long to
share with you, or to simply hear
your laughter, and sometimes, just
for a moment, I forget you are gone.

October 2018 – Ghost

It's been just over three years since you died.
Although I still think about you from time to time
I've realised that it's true what people say.
"A day at a time, life goes on, time heals
everything," and other well intentioned things.
If this is what is meant by healing, it's as though
a thick, hard scab has formed over my feelings.
I want to rip it off, make it raw, make it bleed,
expose the deep wound beneath, because then
you would seem more real to me, more alive,
and not just some shadowy ghost from the past.

February 2019 – Snow Angel

The whole village was at a standstill;
the perfect day for a walk. We trudged
across fields shrouded in wedding veil
white, the crunch of virgin snow underfoot
the only sound in the muffled silence.

Laughter bubbled as we pushed thigh-deep
through snowdrifts sculpted by the wind,
taking photos of wild rose hips, like drops
of bright blood, in the frozen hedgerows
along the railway line.

You lay down in your gorgeous pink jacket,
laughing as you spread your arms and legs
wide, making a snow angel. And now you're
an angel of a different kind, or perhaps you
are a star, shining more brightly than any
other in the galaxy.

(Photo taken in December 2010)

BALL AND CHAIN:

I was asked to submit an assessment piece for a Creative Project whilst doing a Masters in Creative Writing, the Arts & Education at Sussex University as a mature student, during 2001/2002. The local Pantomime Society very kindly allowed me to raid their wardrobe for props and costumes, following which I performed this monologue in front of my tutors and fellow students.

Ball and Chain

Mirror mirror on the wall
Who is the fairest of them all?
God, I look like a great big pumpkin
in this. I should never have listened to
my Fairy Godmother. It feels really tight
and these crystal sling-backs are killing me.
The only good thing about having tiny feet
is that when my stepsisters want to borrow
my Jimmy Choos, they can't fit into them.

Mirror mirror on the wall
Tell me the biggest lie of all
If I hold my stomach in
Will you tell me I am thin?
No…… I guess not.

I asked Buttons earlier, *Now Buttons,*
I said. *I want you to be brutally honest.*
Does my bum look big in this?
And do you know what he said?
I think you look sexier with a few more
curves. In other words, he thinks I'm fat.
So I said, *Well, thanks for nothing.*

He's no Prince Charming himself, is he?
With his thinning hair and his beer gut.
Oh God! I'm going to be late if I don't
get a move on. It won't take me long to
get changed if he'd just stop pestering me.
And if he asks me if it's that time of the

BALL AND CHAIN

month once more, I'll scream!
Patronising bastard.

Right, what shall I wear then?
Maybe the black lace.
It's a bit see through, mutton dressed
as lamb, **she'd** say, but then I never can
get it right. First she tells me I'm too thin.
*You should put some weight on dear,
you look anorexic.* And now it seems
I've gone to the other extreme.
What was it she said the other day?
Oh yes....*You're getting a bit of a bottom
on you, Cinders.* Bloody old witch!
Now where's that red dress?
*Mirror mirror on the wall
Who is the.........***OH SHIT!**
Look at the wine stain.
How about the long velvet skirt
with the white lace top?
Cinderella, you will go to the ball!
She'd approve of this all right. Well,
that's exactly why I'm not going to wear it.
Don't know why I bought it in the first place.
Might as well give it to Oxfam.

I suppose that stuck-up cow with the
long black hair and the perfect
skin will be there. Snow White!
Give me a break! There's a rumour
going round that she sleeps with seven
dwarves. Not that I listen to gossip.
And as for her sister Rose Red,
she's got a thing about bears!

BALL AND CHAIN

Well it takes all sorts.

I bet Snow White will be wearing her
pashmina. I haven't the heart to tell her
that it's so passé! But that won't keep
the best-looking men from buzzing round
her. They'll hang on her every word,
whilst I get stuck with the ones who
just want to talk about themselves.
ALL evening.

And if I'm very lucky, one of them might
get around to asking me *And what do you do
for a living?* Well actually, I sweep floors and
take out the ashes. It's a bit of a conversation
killer. I could always go as one of the ugly sisters.
OH FUCK!..... I've broken a nail. That does it,
I'm not going. It wouldn't have been much good
anyway. Fancy having to be home by twelve
when it's an all night party. I'll just have to say
that I couldn't find any mice.

BELIEF:

I've wanted to write this poem since 1993, when the News Headlines during one week in August were all absolutely appalling examples of man's inhumanity to man. Then, following a conversation with my sister Melly in 2013 about the terrible events taking place in Syria, I finally sat down and wrote it. The first line is taken from the last line of the third verse of a beautiful and moving poem entitled "Italian Beach," which my father wrote whilst stationed in Italy, during the 2nd World War. I have included a copy in the Appendix. I was also inspired by Thomas Paine's quotation: *"My country is the world and my religion is to do good."*

It also seemed appropriate to include the poem **A Grand Day Out** in this section, which I wrote after seeing a news report on the TV.

Belief

Yes, man still hates.
No limit to his inhumanity and indifference,
fuelled by ignorance, rage, a need for drugs,
deprivation, religious fervour, fanaticism,
a basic lack of love or nurture perhaps,
the list is endless.

Yet I don't ask *How can God stand by and
do nothing?* even though it's tempting, when
I know it is us who stand by and do nothing,
smug and snug in our comfortable homes,
lacking nothing, shored up by our possessions.

It's quite possible God made a mistake when
He created the World and entrusted us with it.
He gave us free will, sadly underestimating the
depth of man's greed, his limitless capacity for
hate and violence, and whilst I don't pretend
to know who or what God is, I believe in the
human spirit, and that if we turn our back on
Him, we turn our back on good.

A Grand Day Out

Skegness in January, there's a festive air;
a magnificent sperm whale has beached
itself. Hordes of people gather, laughing,
pointing, posing with their selfie-sticks.
The owner of the ice-cream van can't believe his
luck, kicking himself when supplies run out.
Children clamber over your poor, rotting body,
a man tries to extract one of your teeth, a sick
souvenir, but the worst indignity of all; the CND
Ban the Bomb sign spray-painted on your tail.

FOR MY SISTER: 2019

Big Sister

When you call me today, you start to cry.
You've always been the strong one, so brave
and fearless despite years of battling
illness and pain. But now there's a new
health scare, and you've had enough.
I tell you to hang on in there, everything
will be alright, that I will come.

After I put the phone down, a kaleidoscope
of childhood memories plays out in my head.
I remember how, although we often fought
like cat and dog, you always took care of me, kept
me safe, and I was happy to stand in your shadow.

In the summer holidays, Mum sometimes sent
us off for the day with half-a-crown, a couple of
slices of buttered bread and a hard-boiled egg
with salt and pepper in a twist of greaseproof
paper each, to get us out from under her feet.

You can't have been much more than nine
years old, and me about seven the first time
you took me to the Tower of London, somehow
finding the way by bus, train and tube, clutching
my hand tightly in case we got separated.

BIG SISTER

I remember how enthralled we were, listening to a Beefeater's spine-chilling description of the severed heads impaled on spikes, the two young Princes incarcerated in a cold, damp tower, the one-way journey through Traitor's Gate, and how two of Henry VIII's wives were beheaded there.

You took me to all sorts of wonderful places. Places like Hampton Court Palace, where we got lost in the maze. We fed some of our bread to the ducks at Kew Gardens, climbed 253 steps to the top of the Great Pagoda, then sat by the lake to eat our lunch.

I think about those innocent, happy times, just the two of us together, and wish that I had your courage.

OTHER STUFF:

Pipe Dream

You'll grow more beautiful with age, he says,
cupping my chin in his hand and gazing tenderly
into my eyes, making my insides melt. How is it
then, that he's off like a rat up a drainpipe with a
a new, younger, botoxed squeeze when the first
few wrinkles appear, and my skin begins to sag.

(I wrote this short poem recently, whilst thinking about a boyfriend who, many years ago, said these actual words to me. He was very intense and quite exhausting, so our relationship didn't last long, and it ended amicably. I liked the sentiment, but wanted to come up with a more cynical and amusing take on it.)

Picture This

My mother started to paint in oils in later life, even though she was partially sighted and registered blind. One of my most treasured possessions was the painting she did of a path leading through a wood full of bluebells, which she gave to me after I said how much I loved it. I had it framed and hung it on the wall in my study, so I could gaze at it whilst I was writing. A few months later, she told me she wanted it back, as she hadn't realised that it was also my stepfather's favourite, but it would, of course, be returned to me if either of them died.

I didn't have the heart to take the picture away from Martin, when Mum died in 2005. He said he'd made it clear in his will that it belonged to me, and anyway, we discussed it with his son and daughter during lunch at the Horse & Groom, not long after Mum's funeral. I'd met them several times before, and they seemed pleasant enough. When Martin died nine years later, I left a decent interval before phoning his son to ask if I could have the painting back. He said that he was sorry, but it had somehow been put in a box with other stuff and given to a local charity to be sold in one of their shops.

I was broken-hearted and trawled all the shops in vain, posted on Facebook, emailed local newspapers, offered a reward. The Eastbourne Herald wrote a short piece, appealing for its return, a long shot. I've had to accept that the painting is lost, but I am so bloody angry that neither of Martin's offspring ever expressed genuine regret for what had happened, and I haven't heard a single word from them since that day, not even a card at Xmas.

Nerine

I've been waiting for this moment.
Green shoots thrust through the bleak
October earth, straining towards the
light. Every day I watch them
grow, until at last, delicate pink
flowers emerge from papery cauls,
tremble on the slender stalks.

Not even the hurricane of '87
can uproot her. She sways and
bends to the rhythm of the wind,
whilst all around the arms of
mighty oak trees claw at the sky
in a last macabre dance before
falling, like men after battle.

Samaritan

I am humming as I drive back from
the station. A streak of tabby, a dull
thud. *Oh God, please, no*, I scream.
Pull over. Run back. The cat writhes
in the road doing backward flips and
somersaults, a demented gymnast.
I run up and down the pavement,
sobbing and screaming.

A man comes up to me.
Is there anything I can do?
The cat has stopped moving.
He picks it up, lays it on the verge.
It's all over now. I'm still running
on the spot, shaking uncontrollably
as I scrub at my face with a tissue.

The man stands in front of me.
He doesn't slap my face or tell me
to pull myself together, just holds
my arms so I have to look at him.
It ran right out in front of you.
There was nothing you could do.
I'll take care of everything.

I stare at the fleck of white foam
under his right nostril. He probably
shaved in a hurry before popping out
for the newspaper. I feel an absurd
desire to wipe it away tenderly with the
sodden tissue. *Thank you for being so
kind to me,* I say instead.

Charlie: Postscript to Black & White

I was only 10 when he went missing.
It's just a cat people said, but I felt
as if I'd lost my only friend. He'd sit
in the tree by the front door, jump
down onto my shoulder when I came
home from school, and drape himself
around my neck like a scarf.

I overheard my neighbour telling my Mum
He's not the only one to go missing.
I've heard that cats are being taken for
experiments, you know, and vivisection.
When I found out what it meant I was
haunted for months by images of Charlie
in pain, being tortured, and fifty seven
years later, it still makes me cry.

Aurora

Konrad pulls off the road, kills the lights.
Darkness swallows us up, heavy and
impenetrable. I feel a moment of panic,
remembering the time my sister shut me
in a cupboard and wouldn't let me out.
I think this is the place, he says.
Now we must wait for her.

We stand outside the minibus, staring
at the velvet sky as he points out the
various constellations, then pours hot
chocolate from a thermos. I clutch the
mug in my numb fingers, sip gratefully.
It's minus 8 degrees, and I can no longer feel
my toes, so I stumble back onto the bus.

Suddenly, a shout goes up. *Here she is,
right on cue!* I hurry down the steps,
see an arc of shimmering green in the
purple sky, illuminating a solitary white
building on the horizon. I hear my daughter
gasp, our frozen hands and feet forgotten,
as we watch Aurora dance.

ENDINGS:

Rest in Peace

Poor old Bob. After thirty-five years
of useful service you were dismissed,
thrown out like an old handbag
showing signs of wear and tear.

Years of fixing rooms for lodgers, putting
up with her tantrums and sulks, the trick
we played on you with the stick insect,
all stuffed into three black dustbin bags.

I remember once how the lid flew off the
Heinz ketchup bottle when Melly shook it.
We tried hard not to laugh, afraid of Mum's
reaction, in the stunned silence that followed.

Although you seemed to take it quite well,
just looked at the sauce dribbling down your
shirt, Mum was furious, and gave Melly a
good hiding after you'd gone back to work.

As I got older, you'd sometimes slip me a
ten shilling note, *"Don't tell your mother,"*
then helped me pass my driving test,
worked on my clapped-out mini.

Back then, I thought I hated you for
taking Dad's place, and now, years
later, I wish I could thank you, tell you
that I love you, but it's too late.

V Sign

You lie in the hospital bed,
fettered by tubes and drips.
Lights dance to your beat
on the monitor's screen.

Dry as bark, your fingers fumble;
the photograph of the new baby,
the card your granddaughter made.
Get wel sune.

Later, I walk along the path
bordered with wild garlic and primroses
turning their faces to the sun,
then stop at the gate to your cottage.

In the distance, there's the outline
of the V etched in conifers,
planted on the South Downs
for Queen Victoria's Jubilee.

I think how lucky I am
as I turn my back on
that bloody fuck off V sign
you'll never see again.

Bearhug

She sits in her chair
fretting over the greenfly
on the roses she can no longer smell,
remembering how she once laid a path
of crazy paving all by herself.

And when I say goodbye
I hold her as carefully as a blackbird's
egg, wishing she would pull me onto
her lap, hug me so hard my ribs hurt,
just...one...more...time.

Last Photo

You're sitting on a chair by the bed,
greasy hair plastered to your skull,
the hospital gown several sizes too big.
Susie your granddaughter holds baby Anna,
who has reached out to grasp your hand.
You always had such intense brown eyes
but now they look like marbles as you gaze
at the camera, a wavering smile fixed
on your lined and weary face.

It's hard to believe that we celebrated
your 90th birthday just over a year ago.
You arrived in style, stepping from the
chauffeur driven Rolls Royce, every bit the
lady, looking radiant and regal in your long
slit skirt and high heels as you cut the birthday
cake and gave a speech, the slight stoop of your
shoulders the only hint of the advancing years.
And that is how I want to remember you.

The Magic Book

Once upon a time there lived a King and Queen in a beautiful palace in a far away kingdom. The Queen was clever and beautiful, but she had a terrible temper, and would throw a tantrum if she didn't get her own way.

Well, actually, it wasn't a palace; it was a dilapidated semi-detached in Wandsworth, London. Violet, who had a short fuse at the best of times, complained bitterly about their next door neighbours. "They're as common as muck" she said. "Always shouting and swearing. And have you seen the state of their curtains? It lets the whole street down." Alfred assured her that they would be able to move to a bigger house in a better area within a couple of years.

The King loved his wife very much, and doted on their young daughter, Princess Jasmine, but he had to go away for several years on a quest to defend the realm. One day, Jasmine caught her foot in the hem of her long gown, and fell all the way down the marble staircase in the Great Entrance Hall. There she lay, as still as a statue. Although the Queen summoned the Royal Physician immediately, Jasmine could not be saved. A message was sent to the King, who was distraught when he heard the news. When he returned, he would not speak to anyone for many months, but eventually, the Queen told him she wanted another child. Within a year, their second child was born, a daughter named Princess Mariana. Their third daughter, Princess Juliet, was born nearly two years later, and the King and Queen were very happy now that their family was complete.

Like most couples, Alfred and Violet had a few problems. Alfred had enlisted in the Army at the outbreak of World War II. Whilst he was away in South Africa, their six year old daughter June died in a tragic accident. It was a month before Alfred was able to return home, and June had already been buried by then. There was no such thing as Bereavement Counselling or Marriage Guidance in those days; people were expected to keep a stiff upper lip and muddle through. Violet was delighted when she became pregnant for the second time, and fondly pictured herself cradling a sleeping baby, wrapped in the beautiful white shawl she had lovingly knitted. Her romantic notions were rudely shattered by the fact that Mary was a difficult and fractious baby, who didn't seem to like being cuddled, and only went to sleep if she was put in her cot.

Their third daughter Jane arrived two and a half years later. She was born jaundiced, and her yellow skin and topknot of gingery hair clashed somewhat with the sweet little nightdresses printed with red rosebuds, which Violet had made her. However, she wasn't such a difficult baby as Mary, and slept peacefully in her mother's arms.

The Queen soon became jealous of her daughters because the King loved them so much and spent many happy hours playing with them.

"Don't bother your father children. He's had a hard day at the office" Violet snapped, when Mary and Jane tried to climb onto Alfred's lap as he sat reading the newspaper in his favourite armchair. Alfred didn't take any notice of his wife. He got down on all fours and chased the squealing girls around the living room, pretending to be a bear. Violet watched tight-lipped and tutted loudly until finally she couldn't stand it any longer. "Oh for goodness sake, you're making them too excited and it's giving me a headache." Mary and Jane recognised the warning signs and went upstairs to get ready for bed.

The Queen spent a great deal of time gazing at herself in one of the many mirrors in the Palace, convinced that she was losing her looks. She sent her servants far and wide in search of exotic potions and precious oils and perfumes, which were kept in cut glass phials in her pink and gold boudoir.

Even though they knew they would get into terrible trouble if they were caught, Mary and Jane were fascinated by the mysterious bottles and beauty preparations which jostled for space on their mother's dressing table. The perfumes had exciting names like Evening in Paris, and Moonlight Mist. They removed the lids and inhaled deeply longing for the day when they would be old enough to wear them. Once, Mary was bold enough to try her mother's bright red lipstick but she pressed too hard and it snapped. She and Jane were horrified and hid it hastily at the back of the dressing table drawer, hoping their mother wouldn't notice. "You wicked, ungrateful children" she raged, when she discovered what they had done. She banged their heads together hard and sent them to bed without any tea.

One day the King became very ill. Before he died he summoned the Queen to his bedside.

Mary & Jane's father didn't really die. Violet threw him out when she found a younger, more exciting lover. He moved in the very same day as Alfred moved out. "Say hello to your Uncle Brian, girls" was all she said. Mary and Jane didn't see much of Alfred after that, as their mother either flew into a rage, or sulked for days when she found out they'd been to see him.

"You must guard this book carefully and give it to my precious daughters when they are old enough to appreciate it," the King said, struggling to catch his breath as he handed the Queen a dusty old book with a dull black cover.

The Queen had never seen it before, and when she opened it, she saw that it was written in a strange and unfamiliar language. She was very angry, and threw the book into the bottom of an old, wooden chest which stood in a disused tower in the remotest part of the palace, and there it lay for many years.

Alfred loved reading more than anything. During the 2nd World War he had sent his wife a copy of The Complete Works of Shakespeare all the way from North Africa, after writing a moving inscription on the flyleaf. Violet put it in a cupboard and forgot all about it. She would rather have had a pair of silk stockings or some perfume.

As the years passed the Queen became even more jealous of her daughters, who were kind, loving and gentle. She criticised them constantly, and they could do nothing right.

"It's a pity you're so thin and your hair is as straight as dish water" Violet said to Jane. "It makes your face look even longer." Mary did not escape her mother's vitriolic observations either. "There'll be no more cakes for you," Violet told her. "You're getting too fat. And I do hope your feet don't grow any bigger. It is so unbecoming in a woman." Mary's first attempt at making dinner ended in disaster when the potatoes boiled dry, filling the kitchen with thick black smoke and ruining the saucepan. "You stupid girl, you're totally useless," Violet yelled, pulling Mary's hair and hitting her with the bamboo cane, which always stood in the corner. When Jane tried to stop her, she smacked her hard round the face.

Mariana and Juliet were not allowed to talk to the servants, or to go outside the palace grounds. They were afraid to disobey the Queen, because she flew into terrible rages at the slightest thing, and would beat them, and lock them up without food or water for days. They tried hard to please their mother but she became even more cruel and spiteful.

Violet was highly strung and had unrealistic expectations of her daughters. They might just as well have been princesses for they were

THE MAGIC BOOK

not allowed to behave like normal children who scream and shout and get dirty. "I expect you to behave like young ladies at all times," she told them. On one occasion, they dared to walk along the wall outside their neighbour's house. "Get off that wall this minute," she shrieked. "Why couldn't you have been more like your sister June? She never gave me a moment's worry."

The Queen would not let her daughters play with the village children. Their only friends were the birds who flew down into the garden and took crumbs from their outstretched hands, and allowed them to stroke their soft feathers.

When Mary or Jane ventured to ask if they could invite their school friends to tea she exploded. "Do you think I am made of money? I work my fingers to the bone and this is all the thanks I get" she shouted, banging a saucepan noisily against the worktop for emphasis. They didn't ask her again. They didn't have many friends anyway. The other children made fun of them because they talked 'posh'.

"Ooh look, here comes plain Jane and hairy Mary" they jeered, forming a circle around them in the playground. The two sisters compensated by losing themselves in the imaginary world they created for themselves. Sometimes it was a world in which they became beautiful princesses with parents who adored them and indulged their every whim. At other times, they became famous explorers who swam across crocodile infested rivers and wrestled with man-eating tigers. Jane, in particular, loved reading fairy stories and dreamt of the day when a handsome Prince would gallop up on a white stallion and rescue her.

The Queen set her daughters impossible tasks and told them they were lazy and stupid when they couldn't do them.

"How many times do I have to show you? Can't you do anything right?" Violet screamed, as she ripped the clean sheets and blankets from Mary

and Jane's beds and threw them on the floor. They both struggled to master the complexities of precise 'hospital' corners on the bottom sheets but had failed, as usual, to measure up to their mother's exacting standards.

The palace in which Mariana and Juliet lived stood on a hill in a valley which was surrounded on all sides by towering mountains. The only way out of the valley was over the mountains. They asked the Queen what lay beyond the mountains and she told them that there was nothing but an endless, scorching desert in which nothing could grow, and no one could survive.

*There might just as well have been a mountain between the girls and their freedom. As they grew up their mother warned them of the terrible dangers lurking outside the safety of their home. Men were not to be trusted. They were only after **one thing**, this much the girls knew, even if they weren't at all sure what that one thing was. "Don't go near any bushes and don't talk to any strange men" she'd caution them every time they left the house. They didn't know what their mother meant, but Jane was convinced that voracious animals would be lying in wait for them, and they would be eaten up just like poor Red Riding Hood. Her sister tried to reassure her. "Don't worry, I'll take care of you" she said, and held Jane's hand tightly.*

Mary and Jane's mother undermined her daughters' confidence at every opportunity. She told them they might as well leave school when they reached fifteen. "It's a waste of time and money going on to further education. You're not clever enough and you'll only end up getting married and having babies anyway. You can get a job and start earning your keep."

One day, when the Queen was out riding, Mariana and Juliet decided to explore the palace. They had finished the lessons that their mother had set them, and were tired of all their usual games. Although the Queen had forbidden them to go into the tower because it was dangerous, they climbed up the steep steps and into the room where a wooden chest stood. They pushed the lid up eagerly, and discovered the long-forgotten book. Juliet picked it up and opened it slowly. There was a blinding flash of light, and three snakes as brightly coloured as precious jewels slithered out of the open pages, dropped to the floor and began to glide away smoothly, through the open door. The first snake was as red as ruby, the second as green as emerald, and the third as blue as sapphire. Mariana and Juliet were entranced by their bright colours and quickly followed them, down the stairs, along the corridors and through the courtyard into the garden. As the snakes slid through the palace gate the young princesses did not hesitate, although they knew they would be punished horribly if the Queen discovered them.

They followed the snakes to the foot of the mountains, where they began to glide effortlessly up the steep slopes. Although Mariana and Juliet were afraid, they bravely climbed after them, clinging to the small bushes growing out of the side of the mountain. They climbed and climbed, scratching their hands and knees on the rough surface. After a long time had passed, they reached a small ledge where they rested for a few moments before continuing, until finally, they reached the summit, where they began to look around them. The snakes had disappeared completely, but on the ground a small pile of rubies, emeralds and sapphires lay twinkling brightly in the sunlight. They walked to the other side of the mountain which sloped gently down to lush green fields and woods. Far away in the distance they could see tiny houses dotted about the hillside, and right at the furthest edge of the horizon, a vast expanse of blue and silver. They knew then that their mother had lied to them. They picked up all the jewels and put them in Juliet's bag, along with the magic book, and set off together to seek their fortune in the great wide world outside.

Unfortunately it isn't as simple in real life as it is in fairy tales. It was a few more years before Mary and Jane escaped. When Mary left school she worked in a fish and chip shop for a while. She had endless rows with Violet about the way she dressed, and what time she came in at night. She finally left home after yet another row with her. Mary had always been braver than Jane. She found herself a seasonal job on the Isle of Wight, waiting on tables in a seedy guest house, and became quite skilful after a few mishaps. One day at breakfast, a slice of bacon slid off the plate she was carrying right down the front of a travelling salesman's pristine white shirt, leaving a greasy trail in its wake. Another time, she spilt gravy in a lady's handbag, which was open on the floor. They were very understanding under the circumstances and gave her a large tip when they left. All the guests told the proprietor "Mary's such a lovely girl, always smiling no matter what."

After only one season, Mary found her Prince. Rob was a local boy who worked as a carpenter, making beautiful pieces of furniture. Before long, she found out she was pregnant, so her mother hastily arranged a wedding on the cheap, relieved that no-one she knew in London would be there to witness her shame. Alfred came to the wedding and looked as proud as punch as he gave Mary away. She had two daughters in quick succession, followed by a son, six years later, and resigned herself to a life of nappy washing and eking out the housekeeping for the time being.

Now that Mary had left home, Violet focused all her attention on her younger daughter. "You can wash all that muck off your face. You're not leaving my house looking like a prostitute" she screamed at Jane the first time she wore lipstick and mascara. Jane worked as a sales assistant in Marks and Spencer for a while but standing up all day made her feet ache, so she found a job as an office junior in a small shipping company. She tried to ignore it when her boss, an obese and red-faced man with fingers like fat pink sausages kept pinching her bottom and making comments full of sexual innuendo. However, when he tried to pin her up against the filing cabinets one day, she decided that enough was enough. She was working as a typist at the GLC Supplies Department when she met her own Prince Charming. Jeff was a computer operator and was tall, dark and handsome. He took her for a spin on his Lambretta, showered her with compliments, and made her feel like a beautiful princess. When Jane became pregnant within a few months, she and Jeff eloped to Gretna Green. It was a fairly soulless occasion, even though her father came to the wedding with Violet and "Uncle" Brian.

After a long and painful labour Jane gave birth to a baby girl. Jeff wasn't very pleased when he found out that she was pregnant again two years later. He roared off into the sunset in his rusty Triumph Herald without a backward glance, when the baby, another girl, was nine months old. Jane's father Alfred died a month later, following a heart attack. "I told you men aren't to be trusted" was all her mother said and moved to Spain, where she had bought a small apartment with the proceeds from the sale of the family home. On the day she left, she gave Jane the copy of The Complete Works of Shakespeare which she unearthed when she was clearing out the cupboards, prior to moving. Jane had never seen it before and tears filled her eyes when she opened it and read the words her father had written in his beautiful handwriting;

North Africa

April 1943

To my dear wife

"When day is done and shadows fall, I dream of you."

It was the most precious gift her mother could have given her, and she would always treasure it.

THE MAGIC BOOK

Although Jane was heartbroken when Jeff abandoned her, she had no choice but to raise her daughters alone, and did the very best she could. At least Jeff paid regular maintenance, and saw them every so often.

Mary and Jane supported and encouraged each other over the years. They didn't begin to realise their full potential until they were in their forties, by which time their children had all left home to make their own way in the world. Mary went to University first, and after qualifying, became a social worker helping Young Offenders. She was very good at her job and eventually became a Manager. One night, Jane, who had re-married and given birth to another daughter, had a strange dream about an old book. When she woke up, she realised it was the book her father had sent to her mother during the war. She decided to write a fairy story about her dream. Several years later, the story she wrote helped her to secure a place on a Creative Writing Course at Sussex University, followed by an MA in Creative Writing, the Arts & Education. She hopes to become a successful writer.

Mary and Jane still struggle to make sense of their lives. The most important thing they have learnt is that the journey they began long ago has no ending.

APPENDIX

Italian Beach by A.J. Smith

The waves curve inwards
tossing their white heads and flirting
as they gently kiss the strip of sand
that lies before me.

Sighing softly in repetition deploring
that but one is here to see
the beauty and simplicity of it all.
The wind too sighs, lamenting
of the sun now obscured by ever
deepening banks of clouds
while I watch alone.

Sitting here listening to the music
that nature brings, a discordant note
spoils this splendid symphony.
A war plane passes, a strange bird.
Man still hates.

The buildings inland stand steeped
in silence, their windows eyes brooding
on that quiet beach, too quiet, waiting
for the sound of childish laughter.

A ladybird sits on my hand, closing her
wings delicately as she alights. I murmur
that quaint doggerel learnt of childhood
and gently blow. It falls to the sand, spreads
its wings and bustles away,
leaving me alone.

APPENDIX – ITALIAN BEACH BY A.J. SMITH

The sun bursts forth in radiance,
its warmth caresses my naked back
like the arm of a lover.
Azure sky speckled by wisps of snowy down
scampering away before the breeze.
The sea whispers gently, whispers, whispers.
I sleep alone.

www.ingramcontent.com/pod-product-compliance
Lightning Source LLC
Chambersburg PA
CBHW061454040426
42450CB00007B/1356